Scandal in the
Jungle

Scandal in the Jungle

A True Vietnam Story

Rick Marsh

authorHOUSE®

AuthorHouse™
1663 Liberty Drive
Bloomington, IN 47403
www.authorhouse.com
Phone: 1-800-839-8640

Published by AuthorHouse   05/18/2012

ISBN: 978-1-4772-1025-3 (sc)
ISBN: 978-1-4772-1024-6 (e)

Library of Congress Control Number: 2012909088

CONTENTS

Preface.. vii

1. In The Beginning... 1

2. 1963 Naval Blockaid of Cuba 4

3. The Vietnam Involvement 6

4. December 1966—North Island, San Diego, California—............ 7

5. Black Berets— 18

6. Civil Action 20

7. Water Ski Adventure 23

8. Seal Operations... 26

9. Operation "Robin Hood" 29

10. Operation 'Silver Spoon' 30

11. Motar's To No Where.. 32

12. Shoot Out At The 'Ok Corral' 33

13. Deadly Conseqenses... 34

14. My Hero 36

15. Up Up And Away 38

16. R&R (Rest And Relaxation)...................................... 40

17. Maid Of Honor 43

18. Sunday Excursion 44
19. Disobey Orders.. 46
20. As Fate Would Have It.. 48
21. Airforce Base Fire.. 50
22. On Patrol... 53

PREFACE

This book contains stories of actual events that took place in a one year period, 1967, during the Vietnam War.

The author was the personal aid of the commander of all River Patrol Forces (Patrol Boat River (PBR Forces-Commander Task Force CTF-116) when he was stationed there.

Because he was in direct contact with all the reports that came in from the different units throughout the country, he had first hand knowledge of all the operations that took place and the people who promulgated these reports. In many of these cases, he took part in the operations and saw first hand what happened.

He was then the person who proof read and corrected all reports of the operations that went to the commanding officer for final review and then forwarded to command headquarters in Saigon then on to the White House.

CHAPTER ONE

In The Beginning

To begin this saga I must start with a brief synopsis of my experiences just prior to and after joining the Navy.

After graduation from high school, I could only find one job, picking corn in Cowley Wyoming. My friend and I traveled up pass Yellow Stone National Park and dropped down into this small town which had a cannery for Libby foods. The boss said we had come to the wrong place because he only hires Mexicans to pick corn and peas. Well, we had spent our last cent on gas and rolled down to the factory out of gas. He consented to give us jobs in the factory doing odd jobs for one dollar an hour, working eighteen hours a day with no overtime pay. And. he gave us a place to stay, his daughter's play house, just big enough for two cots and he gave us a hot plate, a pot, and two plates with utensils.

We worked there for the summer then took our pay checks and went back down to Utah and started college with just enough to pay the tuition for one semester. No jobs at college or in the town, money ran out and the semester was over, what next, Join the "Navy", which I did in May 1959.

When I joined the Navy, I weighed 118 pounds and was 5 feet ten inches tall. A lack of milk at home I supposed. After 9 weeks in boot camp and allowed to drink all the milk I wanted and eating great food and ice cream, I gained two inches and forty two pounds. Nobody recognized me at home when I went there for 30 days leave after boot camp.

In 1959, I got orders to report to Port Hueneme, Sea Bee Base, in Oxnard, California to the Staff office. After one year, my time was up and I applied for the Submarine School in Connecticut. I took a 30 day leave due to the death of my step father and when I returned the Personnel man failed to forward my request for sub school and I had received orders to report too the Naval Reserve Training Center, Honolulu, Hawaii. I had no idea what this was but it sounded ok being in Hawaii. When 1 arrived, I was assigned as Yeoman in charge of the Surface Division (Reserve) which meant meetings twice a week. I took care of all the paper work for this unit and attended each reserve meeting from 6 to 9 each Tuesday and Thursday nights. 1 had duty only once a month at the Center so I had a lot of time to enjoy Hawaii. I was told there was no billet for a single sailor at Pearl Harbor, so I had to rent an apartment off the Center. There was one other Yeoman there who was single, so he and I rented a place near Waikiki next to the Alawai Cannel. We were the only "White" guys there, the rest of the people in the apartment complex were "local", Hawaiian and other races.

After about two months living there, I wanted to learn how to surf, so I asked some local kids if they would teach me. They said ok but first I had to buy a surf board. Having very limited money after paying the rent and bus fair back and forth to work, told them how can I afford one. Well, they found one for $40.00, twelve foot balsa wood and all beat up. I got it and they had me paddle across the Alawai Cannel and to the other side too Waikiki Beach. After several months and two more boards, I became pretty good and was able to by a 1950 Ford convertible to carry the board in. Me and 4 local kids from ages 14 to 17 began traveling around the island and surfing and sleeping on the beaches on the week ends.

I still wanted to go too Church and meet some girls my own age and race, So, after 6 months I was able to go to a Seminary Class for high school kids near my work place. Man was I happy, the class was full of young girls. 14 to 18 and all different races. Their parents were both local and military, hence the mixed races. I began to court them, one at a time, taking them to dances and entertainment activities in town. Almost two years went by and I found my future wife to be. She was just turning 17 and I was 22, a small problem for her parents. After a family meeting and promises by me to have her finish high School, they allowed our marriage in 1962.

After I got married, I was transferred to CINCPACFLT, Commander in Chief of the Pacific Fleet, located just outside Pearl Harbor up on a hill. There, I was assigned to the Operations Division, where I typed Top Secret and lower messages and reports for the 4 star Admiral. At that time, Vietnam had not been a US interest. However, Communist Russia was a problem and I found out what a big problem they were.

CHAPTER TWO

1963 Naval Blockaid of Cuba

After working until October 1963, one morning a Marine Lieutenant came into my office and said I was to lock up all my safes and follow him. I thought I had lost some Top Secret stuff or something so I was scarred stiff. I locked up and followed him out of the building, where there were 15 to 20 cars lined up with all the Yeoman being put into the cars.

We were driving out to the Sugar Cain fields and drove into a gravel pit. There I was asked for my Kunia Card. "What was that" I explained to the Marine Sergeant who met me at our car. I found it in my wallet and he then told all of us to walk toward these great big steel doors going into the mountain. At every door we went thru there was a Marine asking for our ID's. Finally, down one hallway I was led through a door and to my surprise there was a long table with several officers surrounding it and using push sticks to move little replica of ships around the table near a fake island. Over in the comer was another officer, reading what looked like message to a television camera.

All this time we were told not to talk to anyone except the guards. I was led to another back room where I was told to take one typographic message off this machine and put it into another, then take out and place it in the file box next to that officer reading the messages to the TV.

After glancing at the decoded messages I was handling, I noticed the words, Block aid, Communist, Russia, Cuba, President Kennedy, Missiles,

I was sure we were about to have World War III and I was down a mile deep in the ground with my wife and kid above ground.

They said they had called our families and told them we were not coming home for a while and that we were OK. After 8 hours of this, we were finally taken to a room and given an explanation what was going on. A block aid of Cuba, because the Russians had nuclear missiles on Cuba and they were aimed at the US and that we here in Hawaii were running the block aid of any more Russian ships carrying these missiles heading for Cuba, for fear that Washington could he hit by missiles.

In an adjacent room, there was the top brass from every service. watching the reports on TV and sending out orders to the Table and by Top Secret Messages to those ships to move here or there for the effect of the block aid. They also had the "Red Phone" talking straight to the President to keep him informed. Meanwhile, there were spy planes flying over the area to give us up to date data.

As the world new, 3 days later, Kruchev gave in and started moving the missiles out of Cuba and we were allowed to go home for a few days.

CHAPTER THREE

The Vietnam Involvement

President Kennedy had given the South Vietnamese and the French a number of "Advisors" to fight the North Vietnamese, but that was all the involvement we had there.

After Kennedy was killed, and Johnson became president, the French were getting out after 20 years of fighting. Then there was that infamous missile attack in the Gulf of Tonkin on one of our destroyers (huh). This of course led us to going into a War footing in Vietnam.

At first, the Navy was asked to provide volunteers to serve in an area in the country, but as I will explain, this changed to automatic orders instead of "volunteering".

Only two months later, my wife and I and one child were given orders to San Diego Naval Repair Facility. I would be the only Yeoman assigned there along with three officers. The rest of the personnel were civilians. After one year there, I was transferred to the Naval Personnel Office on the North Island Naval Air Station across the bay. I was put in charge of the Benefits and Awards section. I was there for another year and was then transferred to AMD, Aircraft Maintenance Division on the same base. It was there I got my orders to Vietnam and this is where I will start my saga of "Scandal in the Jungle".

CHAPTER FOUR

December 1966—
North Island, San Diego,
California—

My name is Rick March, 28 year old Navy Second Class Yeoman stationed here as Yeoman in charge of the Medal and Benefits section. Having attended 2 administrative schools, I was trained to type and supervise an office of other yeoman and other Navy Personnel. I had been stationed here for 4 years and was awaiting my new orders at any time. I anticipated orders to a ship because, having been assigned to shore duty for this long period of time the Navy see's to it that you will get sea duty sooner or later.

The Vietnam war had just been escalated by President Johnson and volunteers were being sought to do a I year tour in Vietnam. At mail call, I got a letter of assignment from PAMI, the office of assignment for Sailors serving in the Pacific. Anxiously. I opened the letter and began reading out loud so my shipmates, who had gathered around me to here where I was being assigned. To my surprise and utter disappointment it read "You have been ordered to serve 1 year in Vietnam. Report to Camp Pendleton on 15 Dec for SERE Training and wait for further orders". "Man alive, I didn't volunteer for this what the heck is going on here I said". One of the office personnel, a Personnel Man Third Class by the name of Bob, one of my best friends spoke up, "hey I volunteered, and maybe I'll get my orders soon". I wasn't too happy about it as I had a wife and two kids and one on the way any day now. How was I going to explain these orders to her, after all we had talked about this possibility several times?

Suddenly, I had a great idea. "Bob, since you volunteered for this kind of duty, why don't you and I go down to the PAMI Office, which was only a block away, and see if they will change my orders to you and give me some other orders, after all, my orders must be some mistake".

No luck, as soon as we got down there, the Yeoman in charge of assignment sympathized with me but said new orders had came from Washington saying "All Navy Personnel will be assigned a tour in Vietnam effective immediately, President Lyndon Baines Johnson". Bob was delighted and I was peed off. I told Bob I hope Richard Nixon gets in there and stops this war.

I began making up stories and rehearsing what I was going to tell my wife. I took off on my Honda scooter I used to go to work on and arrived home a little late, about 5:00 PM. I gave her my usual greeting of "hi honey, how was your day, is the baby still kicking?" Well, she was understandably tired and answered with a slight smile and a nod as she continued cooking dinner. She knew something was up as I was late getting home and my demeanor was a lot happier than usual. "Guess what? I said, "What" she answers, I'm going to take a little trip". "A trip, what do you mean, you know we can't afford any trip, besides you know I'm ready to have a baby". "Well, the Navy gave me orders today and I was really mad". "Where did they give you orders too?" Vietnam", "Vietnam, what", oh no, what am I going to do when baby comes? I'm as mad as you are, that stupid Johnson did it, I know he would screw up sooner or later. I am glad your Dad got stationed her in San Diego from Hawaii and we are now living together as a family".

15 December soon arrived and I was off too Camp Pendleton Marine Base in California. When I arrived, I started extensive weapons training. I didn't understand the reason for all the training in heavy weapons, such as 50 caliber machine guns, mortar's, and hand grenades, I figured all I would be firing was a typewriter.

The training was intense and fairly routine until one night a group of men with green painted faces burst into the barracks, carrying M-16's, dressed in black pajamas and wearing oriental reed hats and demanded we all put our hands on our head and file out into the night.

Well, it seemed kind of corny at first, but when one of our group resisted, he was slapped to the ground and tied up. I felt a twinge of fright go through my toes. They commanded all 18 of us to march off with our hands tied behind our backs and rope tied to each of our necks, linking us in a line and blind folded us. We stumbled through the dark being careful not to fall down for fear of hanging by one's neck. Finally, after about what seemed an all night march, we arrived in the middle of a little valley, where you could hear water running. They took off our blind folds and we saw a little pond and in the middle of it was what looked like a bamboo raft.

They then untied one of us and led him out to the raft in chest high water, then to our surprise, opened up the top of this raft which turned out to be a cage like device sunken in the water so only the top was visible. They untied my buddy's hands and through him in the cage and closed the lid. There he was, just enough room for him to keep his head above water and the water was cold.

Next, they marched the rest of us over a hill to an area where they had a bunch of black metal boxes that looked like two door lockers, about 7 feet long, like we had in our barracks. They then told us to strip all our clothes off and placed each one of us lying down in the boxes and closed and locked the doors. There we laid, cold, naked and for me at least, scared out of my wits. I thought a bunch of "Jar Heads" had gone nuts and were taking out their frustration on a few dumb sailors. I must have fallen asleep for a few minutes, when all of a sudden a loud banging noise jerked me awake as they were banging on the metal doors with something hard, a defining sound, as I screamed and kicked back against the sides of the box. This would go on for several minutes at a time then stop. Then one of them would say "Yankee, where is your group?, how many are there?, what's your commander's name?". Finally, it dawned on me, they were putting us through mock prisoner of war games, crap, I was mad, but' reasoned they were trying to prep us for possible capture by the enemy. I never could play the game, hollered out my name, rank and serial number only.

This harassment continued until day brake. When they finally let us out, to our surprise, a "gee dunk" (food) truck was there with a generous supply of hot chocolate and coffee with all the donuts we could eat. They explained they had to surprise us and make it as real as possible so we can be prepared before going to Vietnam and the distinct possibility of being captured and tortured for information.

After a day's rest, we went for a night drill when C-130 Air Force planes called, "Dragon Ships" by the Vietnamese, because when they fired the three Gatlin Guns out the side of the plane they tracers looked liked three long red lines coming down to the ground, came over the sky line. They could put a bullet an 1 inch apart for twenty yards and firing a tracer every seventh bullet and firing four thousand rounds a minute it surely did look like a "Dragon".

The only concerning thing to me was the plane had to fly at a 200 foot altitude and at a 30 degree bank to fire, thus being susceptible to ground fire of the smallest weapons, like a BB gun.

Finally, after two weeks of bad "Jar Head" chow, sleepless nights, brief but convincing "War Games", we were sent home just in time to celebrate Christmas.

Me and my Honey, two kids and a few assorted relatives, spent Christmas together, opening presents, eating "Good" food and trying to pretend it was a joyful occasion, but deep down all but the kids were aware that I would be leaving the next day, which made the celebration of the Lord's birthday take on a new meaning.

I hadn't had much time to reflect on just what I was going to be subjected to in "Nam". Television news casts were more closely watched, names & location of areas, language, all started to play in the conversations. Soon, it became apparent that me and my wife needed to be alone so the relatives left and we put the kids to bed and returned to a night of sleeplessness, tears and expressions of love.

The morning came all too soon and I readied myself and my wife woke the kids and prepared what she feared might be my last breakfast at home. I felt her fears and tried to relieve the tension by making jokes about the hole in my sock and saying to her, "when I get back, you ought to have all my socks mended".

Well, now it was time to go, so her Dad & Mom got up and we all climbed in his old 58 Chevy Wagon, rusty in spots from its long stay in the Hawaiian sea air before being shipped to San Diego. I commented, "I'm going miss this ole Chevy". There was silence most of the ride to San Diego Airport, broken only by the occasional whimpering of my wife and the kids asking why was mommy crying.

We arrived at 8:30 a.m. on the 26th of December. A long hug for the kids & their grand parents, a tender caring hug and kiss for mom with a final comment "I love you, take care of yourself, the baby and the kids and we will see you in 12 months," then off I ran to the plane. As the plane taxied down the runway I could see my young family standing in the air port window, waving hands and throwing kisses. I tried to keep my composure among all the other service men on board, but the thought this may be the last time I may see them and maybe never see our new baby, was too much and I broke down and cried as the sound of the jets muffled out the sound as we roared down the runway and up and away to "Frisco".

I arrived at the San Francisco Airport that morning at 10:00 a.m. I soon found out that we were not the only group leaving. There were thousands of Army, Marines, Airmen and Sailors waiting to board the C-141 Cargo plane to "Nam".

While hanging around the airport, I met a few Navy guys who, as I would later find out, would actually be stationed with me in our final destination. First, there was Seaman Johnson, a 19 year old from Philadelphia, who was a calm and reserved young man about 6 feet tall, single, dark crew cut hair and average build.

Next, there was Norman Small from Brooklyn. A devout Catholic who had studied to be a priest, just married two weeks, and very tense. He was of Italian and Jew decent with a nose to prove it. It turned out that Norm's claim to fame was that he once sang with the group "Four Seasons" on the street corners of Brooklyn before Frankie Valli had joined them and gone on to become real famous. Later on, we all got to hear his great tenor voice as he would hold his tooth brush like a mike and sing to us in our dorm.

Finally, the last one who was to become our leader in the office, Yeoman First Class Riswald. A balding, skinny and very pale guy who had a great ability to memorize anything he read. This turned out to be a problem as he would tell us story after story with a hint of truth.

First, he told a story how he was a professional bowler and averaged 235 per game bowling right handed. Then, one day he was involved in a car accident and broke every bone in his body. When he recovered, he had to switch to become a "lefty" and his average only dropped to a 220 pins per game average. Next, he became a semi-pro tennis player and was sponsored by the Wilson Tennis Ball company. They even made him a custom Jock Strap.

Next, he built a race car which was so fast it could go from the bottom of Indiana too the top in two hours. So fast, even the Highway

Patrol couldn't catch him, even using their radio's didn't help. He was so convincing that he could recite every detail about that powerful engine he built, right down to the details. All this, and much more. Before he joined the Navy he was a chicken farmer. This last revelation was the most believable because he looked like and had legs skinny as a chicken.

6:00 p.m., 16 Dec, we finally boarded the C-141. We were stuffed together like sardines sitting on a make-shift seats consisting of crossed canvas straps so close together your knees were hitting the guy in from of you. 400 guys in an area only meant for 300 at most and this was a cargo plane not a troop carrier.

Anyone sitting next to fuselage at 60 thousand feet high, got pretty cold with only a blanket used as insulation.

The trip would be a 20 your miserable junket with stops at Guam, Midway, Philippines, Tokyo and finally Tan Sa Nut airport outside Saigon, Vietnam. When we finally arrived, our welcome was anything but pleasant, the airport was under mortar attack as we began to land. We made the landing and came to a sudden halt some several hundred yards from the terminal. To avoid the mortar rounds, we were orders to disembark the plane and run to the sand bag bunkers surrounding the terminal. We all ducked our heads and ran, reaching the bunkers and laid there until the mortars stopped and the "all clear" was given.

What a welcome, the whole area was blacked out, just a few red lights here and there so you could find your way to the busses waiting for us. All the windows were painted black on the busses. If you needed to go the bathroom, well, I had no need as I had already peed my pants. We were shuttled to some make shift barracks and told to keep quite and get some sleep.

Sleep! Huh! The noise was unbearable, trucks, motor scooters of every kind, zooming by, honking making every noise you might here at noon in downtown Hong Cong, dust, smoke and smells of sweat, pee and increment insulted the air. I forgot to mention that on the streets people were sleeping on rolled out mats, women squatting in the gutter, men standing there urinating, all without shame or care who was around or looking.

I remember when we first arrived in country, going to the hotel in the morning there was this large grassy field and there were people squatting down so all you could see is the their bamboo hats. I asked someone what they were doing and got a smart answer of "if you had no toilet to go too, where would YOU go?" Hence, we humans do what we got too do when its time to" doodoo"! It reminded me when I used to go to work for my uncle on his alfalfa farm and all he had was an out-house with a copy of a Sears catalog hanging on the wall to wipe with.

At day break, we were hustled off to a Hotel in Saigon where we stayed until receiving orders to go somewhere. For men who were used to clean, calm surroundings of America, any where in America, this was like a waiting room in Hell. No clean clothes, no showers, sea rations for 4 days was par for that course. This hotel had been trashed and the only power we had was from an Army generator which lighted Red Lights at night so you couldn't read anything, welcome to war.

At last, 4 of us got our orders to Binh Thuy "PBR" base, 80 miles south of Saigon. We were each issued an M-1 rifle and a 45 pistol as we left Saigon. We didn't know what PBR meant until we got there. We were flown down there in a twin engine cargo plane and landed at Binh Thuy Air Force Base, about a mile from our base. I was surprised at what we saw as a base, a collection of 4-200 foot long buildings resembling a motel right next to the Bassac River. In between each row of rooms were 2 Sand Bagged bunkers about twenty feet long and 10 feet high with two door openings on each side, with the roof completely covered in sand bags, these were there for us to run too and hide until an all clear siren was blown. The Viet Cong would occasionally mortar our base so we had to hide in these bunkers.

The base was surrounded with barbed wire fences about 10 feet high with 25 foot watch towers at each corner which were manned 24-7 by PBR personnel. There was a large 3 story Navy Barge, an LSD, moored on the river next to the shore, leaving enough room between the Barge and the bank to moor about 20 of these PBR's.

We were taken to our offices which were several rooms at the front end of these buildings with the rest of the building divided into double rooms with a bath area in the middle to house the officer and enlisted Staff, which is what we were, enlisted staff of "Game Warden". To my surprise, each room was assigned a Vietnamese Maid to clean the room and do our laundry. We had to pay them 100 P-asters (their money) equal to 1 dollar American, a day. They were brought to the base everyday from Can Tho and they had to leave every day at 5:00 pm.

Another surprise was every day at noon to 2:00 pm, there was a "Siesta Time" in Vietnam. The War stopped and everyone took this time out to take a nap. On our base all the staff laid out on cots and got a tan for those two hours. The Vietnamese all took naps, including our Maids, who took advantage of our beds and slept in them.

We were introduced to the commanding officer, Captain White, who was dressed in kaki clothes and had a civilian six shooter on his hip, with an Australian Bush Hat on. A wake up call for us that this outfit was a make-shift outfit and that they made up their own rules as they went along, including dress codes. The Captain gave us our job assignments and said go change from those dress blues into Kaki clothes we would get from the supply store. I asked what PBR meant? He laughed and said." Well, it means Patrol Boat River, that's what our job is here to patrol the rivers of the Delta and look for Viet Cong Boats and Sampans running guns and ammunition across the river. By the way, because we don't have any Boatswain Mates trained from the States to be Boat Captains, you will be commandeered for that job until they arrive. Seeing you are a Second Class and have leadership skills, that's what you will be doing for now instead of typing". Ah! We aren't trained either! I sheepishly explained. "Don't worry, we will give you a run down before you go out on the 14 hour patrols".

A brief description of these "boats" is in order. They were converted civilian foam and fiberglass boats about 31 feet long. They had two 220 horsepower General Motors engines which use a water jet pump for propulsion. It's armed with twin .50 caliber machine guns forward and one .50 caliber gun aft, with one M-79 grenade launcher, a 60 MM machine gun and the boat captain has a M-16 rifle. It has a crew of 4 enlisted men and 1 boat captain.

They always travel 2 boats on a mission, one behind the other and can travel at 30 knots. They have radar on board to search down river at night and they also have search lights to light up the enemy for more accurate shooting.

The crews are not supposed to start shooting when they find a suspected boat, but to use the radio and call in the "Sea Wolf" helicopters to come and fire on them. This is unless we are fired on first (known as a fire fight) and if the enemy will be across the river before help comes, then we are authorized to fire. We also call in the Air Force C-130 "Dragon Ships" to get in on the action. These C-130 planes had 3 Gatling Guns on one side of the plane that could fire 4,000 rounds per minute, placing l round every inch for 50 yards. They had tracer bullets at every seven bullets, so at night it looked like 3 streams of fire coming down to the ground, hence the name "Dragon Ships" was given them by the Vietnamese.

During the day time patrols, we signal the Sam Pan's to stop by waving at them to come over to us or fire a barrage of M-16 rounds across their bow. When the Sampans come to us, we search them for weapons, etc, and check their ID Cards. All legal South Vietnamese are required to get ID Cards. If they don't stop after several warning shots, we are authorized to fire the 50's and blow them out of the water. I was used to shooting at birds and animals back home, but to pull the trigger on a human being was going to be a challenge to my morale fabric, yet when it came to self preservation, I hoped I could pull the trigger. This was our orientation before going out on patrols.

Occasionally, we would take Navy Seals on one of their special operations, as they were stationed on our base too. However, they had their own chain of command and our commander had no say over anything they did or any of their personal actions on the base.

When I wasn't on patrol, I was expected to be in the office typing up operations and other classified documents as I was cleared for Top Secret as was all the staff yeoman and officers. The main objective of 'Game Warden" was to stop Viet Cong from infiltrating the Delta via rivers.

The Air Force and Army had their assignment to do the same thing except they were on foot patrols and in the Air. The Army was stationed in a town 5 miles down river named Can Tho and the Air Force had their own base, Binh Thuy Air Base, with a combination of Vietnamese Airmen flying world war II prop jobs, a C-130 gun ship with 3 Gatlin guns on one side, and a couple of L-19 spotter planes as seen in the following illustrations.

In addition, they had several Helicopters, but not jets, as the runway wasn't long enough to accommodate them. There was a night curfew placed on all shipping on the river from 8:00 pm to 6:00 am, so we patrolled with radar looking for violators who would most likely be V.C. There was only one road from Can Tho to our base and also up to Saigon, so the rivers provided the majority of transportation. Also, a lot of the Vietnamese lived on boats and Sampans.

The river ran pretty fast out towards the ocean and it was the color of Brown. The reason for the color is that those living on the river used it as a bathroom and those living on the banks had "out houses" on the banks and did there thing in the rivers. They would even sit there and fish sometimes.

Within a month, we had a change of command, and Captain White was replaced by Captain Doolittle, a former World War II and Korean Pilot. His orders expressly permitted him to only observe by use of a Helicopter but was forbidden to go aboard PBR's or ashore in VC territory. He right away picked his staff and he picked me as his personal secretary/aid. My job was to screen all reports coming from operations throughout the command and make sure they were typed correctly by the other Yeoman in the office before giving them to him for review and forwarding to General Morland in Saigon. I was also given orders from his Chief of Staff, Commander Jones, that when the Captain is in his car that I was driving and he mentioned he whished he had this or that item, I was to go to Saigon and get the item from the Supply Office up there for him.

Later on, this led to me getting a very unusual item that will lead to some controversy. Meanwhile, I got a number of items, film, camera, projector, and various other personal items for him.

The Captain wanted to change the command's name from "Game Warden" to CTF-116, meaning Command Task Force 116. This required a new design for the insignia for our uniforms and hats. After he and the staff designed the insignia, I was told to go to Saigon and find a Vietnamese craftsman to make the insignia out of both cloth and metal. I did exactly that and they made the metal ones out of used tin cans.

Two months after Captain Doolittle took over, a new base was begun about 1 mile down from our old one. The Seabees came in and began building on a blank piece of ground we got from the Vietnamese Governor. It was finished in two months and we moved in. Now we had an open barracks instead of private rooms, so it was not as comfortable as before. We got inventive and hung up ropes and put curtains on them between each man's bunk and locker to get a little privacy. We no longer needed private Maids to clean rooms, so about 4 maids were picked to clean our barracks and the Navy paid for them. I kept my Maid, about 50 years old, to do my clothes and paid her anyway.

CHAPTER FIVE

Black Berets—

The authority to wear a black beret came about when the commanding General of the Vietnamese Army in Can Tho came to Captain Doolittle and asked him to authorize the wearing of the Beret as a symbol of the PBR crews clearing the rivers of most of the Viet Cong and Gangsters. Captain Doolittle asked me to type a letter to the Chief of Naval Personnel in Washington asking permission to change our uniform code for the PBR operations only. There had not been a change in uniform codes for over a 100 years, so we didn't know if it would be approved.

We got the letter of approval and was ordered to get the required number of Berets for all of CTF-116 personnel as soon as possible. I was ordered to find the Berets somewhere in country. I found a local Taylor who had a bunch of them left over from the French occupation before we took over the war effort.

I had to go to each River Group and ask for hat sizes and what number. The Berets had French size hats with numbers 58, 59, etc, so it was a challenge to get enough berets with proper sizes.

The Taylor had to order the other 500 or so berets from France, so it took a while to get enough berets for all the commands. Some of the Helicopter pilots didn't want to wear them at first, but Captain Doolittle put out an Order that all personnel of CTF-116 were to wear them from now on.

I also had to get the proper size cloth and metal insignia's made up again. Wearing these berets became a very big honor and as time went on, even other sailors not associated with CTF-116 wanted to wear them but, were forbidden.

CHAPTER SIX

Civil Action

May 1967, I was asked by a friend, who was stationed there as a civilian for a group called USAID (a front for the CIA), if I would volunteer to teach English, at night time, to Vietnamese in the town of Can Tho at a local school there. By then I was pretty much settled into my job and had lots of time at night to my self so I said yes.

I have never been a teacher, let alone of English, so he gave me a book that was used in South America by USAID workers to teach English.

Norm and I both volunteered and we went there 4 nights a week by driving a jeep to town and started to teach. All my students were Women, 18 and over, except for 5 monks dressed in orange sheets. This class was the very beginning of English for them.

After 3 months, they would graduate to a higher class and keep going until they knew enough to get jobs on American bases. At first I had a hard time relating to them, so I began with basics by drawing on the black board pictures and words and repeating to them and having them repeat back. I hadn't realized there are several words expressing Woman, girl, mother, sister, grandmother, try to draw a picture of just one and how she relates to others.

Later on, I was able to get a tape recorder and began having them speak into the mike and play it back to them so they could here themselves, I got a lot of laughs.

I would take my 45 pistol to class, cock it and lay it on my table so everyone there felt safe. Apparently, a VC had gotten into the school grounds and threw a grenade into one of the class rooms before I started teaching.

It was a little nerve racking driving back to the base at night, as the one road had no lights and lots of bamboo and grass along the road for VC to hide in. The VC came out of hiding at night and wore black pajamas to hide themselves. During the day time, VC were intermingled with everyone else so you didn't know them from anyone else.

One night coming back to base, someone through something at our jeep and hit the hood and bounced off. A wake-up call, to be on the look out, as we drove with our guns at the ready. I taught there until I left country.

Every Sunday, I would go to Binh Thuy Air Base and attend a religious service. One day when coming back to base I noticed a bunch of kids out in a field where the base would dump their garbage. It looked like they were scrounging through cans looking for something to eat. I stopped my jeep and walked over to them and to my surprise, there were 15 boys and girls, some as young as 1 years old. I tried to communicate with my limited Vietnamese I had learned from my Maid and from students at school, I found out they were all orphans, their parents had been killed (coci dow) and they were on their own with one boy as their leader. He was about 11 years old and they all were barely clothed, rags hanging off their little bodies. I felt bad they didn't have much to eat accept the garbage left over in the dump so I told them to all follow me and they walked behind my jeep for a half mile to the base. I went straight to the chow hall and had them come in and sit on the benches. The mess cook was furious, but when I explained their situation he agreed to feed them left over's. I went to Captain Doolittle's room and asked him for permission to help the orphans anyway I could and he said ok.

I found some used clothes from the men on base and went to town and purchased some little clothes for the others. I brought some tents and cots and set up a little place in a empty field close to the base and had them all stay there. Some of the men on base began helping me to feed them and play some games with them when they had time. We had adopted some orphans. Finally, I was able to locate an orphanage in Can Tho where we could take these kids to stay permanently.

While I was Captain Doolittle's driver, I would take him to the Air Force Base where he and the Commanding Officer of the Air Base would play tennis during this Siesta time.

Another time when an Admiral came to visit the base, I took both Captain Doolittle and the Admiral on a Boston Whaler we had which had a 60 caliber machine gun mounted up front. This boat is used to medivac injured Vietnamese to local a hospital from off the river or its banks. But, on this occasion, Captain Doolittle wanted to show the Admiral how safe the river had become since he took over the command. I was the driver and those two were sitting behind me.

After going down river to Can Tho, we turned for home and about half way there a huge rain storm came over us and I could not see anything so I slowed boat and kept it even with the current. We stayed there for 30 minutes before it let up and I could continue. While we were sitting there, the Admiral made a comment to Captain Doolittle "you got this place so secure you could water ski on it."

Remembering what the Chief of Staff told me about getting anything I heard the Captain would say, I decided to go up to Saigon Supply and order a pair of water skis, a floating vest, and rope. The Supply Sergeant was very upset with me this time because I had ordered all this other stuff for the Captain and what was I going to do with water skis? I told him the Captain wanted them so all I am doing is following orders.

CHAPTER SEVEN

Water Ski Adventure

The skis and vest and rope came in about month later and the Sergeant called me and said "your stupid stuff is in".

I went up to Saigon and got the skis and went to the big building that troops waited to be sent around the country. As I walked in, it was very noisy, until they all turned and looked at me holding the white skis, then it got very quite and I felt stupid holding water skis and here they were fighting a war. I quickly went over the transfer desk where I ordered a helicopter to take me back to Binh Thuy and told the desk sergeant to please hide these skis behind his desk until my helicopter arrives. I usually get a ride on a gun ship back to base but after 12 hours of waiting and when the entire building had been emptied, my ride came. It was a Bell two man helicopter and when I got in I could barely fit the skis in with me.

We flew at 50 miles an hour so the chance of getting shot down was evident, hence the reason the pilot didn't fly until very late at night.

After I got back, I slept for about 4 hours, then, woke up two of the Yeoman in my barracks, told them to come with me and get in the Boston Whaler as I was going to try out the skis and make sure the 40 horse Johnson motor would support a skier.

After we went down the Bassac and after getting down a ways, I put on the vest, grabbed the skis and jumped in the water. I told Norman when I was ready for him to hit the throttle all the way down and I would try to get up. Now, I had only skied one time before so I wasn't very prepared to ski this time.

Well, Norm took off and I struggled a bit, then stood up and I was off. It was great, I went down the river running back and forth across the wake of the boat and pulling back and forth with a lot of speed.

Just down the river, I saw a big passenger type Sampan crossing the river with about 50 people on board. I signaled Norm to go close to them and I would fly by, and turn, spraying them with my skis as I sped by. Too my knowledge, no one had ever water skied in Vietnam before so this would be a first for the passengers to see someone flying over the river on skis. We made the pass and I sprayed them and they all waved and yelled their approval.

Later on, as we were coming back up the river, that same San Pan was crossing back across and I told Norm to do it again and as I pulled the rope and flew across toward the Sampan, a man stood up on top and grabbed a long bamboo poll, he must have used to push off the boat when leaving the shore line, and swung at me and I had to squat down and duck, so I let go of the rope and went flying into the bushes next to the shore. He missed me and the people on board all laughed as I went shooting by. Norm pulled the boat back over toward me in the bushes and I grabbed the rope and got back up and off we went again.

During this experiment, I asked Norm and Johnson who were with me if they wanted to try to ski? Johnson said he couldn't swim and declined but Norm said he would try. So after a few instructions on how to put the ski's up and how to hold the rope, I took off and after several tries, he got up and skied for a short distance then quit.

I got back on the skis, and as we approached our base I could see what seemed to be the entire base, including the Captain, standing and waving for me to come in. So I ski'd to the shore just past the LSD where I pulled around and dropped off and floated to the shore.

Captain Doolittle was furious and told me to follow him to his office as the rest of the sailors were all laughing. I marched (soaking wet) back behind the Captain to his office. "What the hell do you think you are doing?" he asked. He said he had gotten calls from every base up and down the river and even the Admiral from Saigon had called to see what was going on. I was gone for 4 hours down the river so I guess there was time for all those calls to come in.

After he had chewed me out for what seemed like an eternity, he said, "what have you got to say" "Well, sir, I said, remember that time you and the Admiral and I were down river on that little excursion and we got rained on pretty bad?" "Yes, well the Admiral made a comment that you had cleaned up the river so good that you could water ski down here. Well, your chief of staff told me that anything you would say in my presence that you might want, I should get it for you. So, I went to Saigon and got the skis and vest and rope and decided to try them out before giving them to you to try". "Oh my hell, the Admiral was only kidding, you son of a gun, take those skis, vest and ropes and lock them somewhere and I don't want to see them every again". "Yes Sir," I said, and walked out and locked them up in a broom closet in our command center. He laughed as I left and I knew I was honest in my getting these skis so he wouldn't punish me in any way.

CHAPTER EIGHT

Seal Operations

The Seals, who were on our base, saw me skiing and thought they would try it too, so they broke in my closet and stole the skis and went skiing behind one of their very fast boats they used for their operations. The Captain found out about it and ordered me to get those skis when they are done and saw them up in the repair shop, which I did.

No more skiing at our base and anywhere else I knew of, while I was in country.

Speaking of the Seals—They wanted to go on an operation using our PBR's down river. They had a meeting with the two boat crews and the Captain, and since I was going along too, I was invited to the meeting.

They discussed what they were going to do based on a Vietnamese that they had captured and had told them where there was a Viet Cong Village. They were going to swim in to the shore at that base location under cover of complete darkness. They were then going to sneak through the bushes and position themselves next the path leading to the their village and when the VC would walk along the path to go out on their little operations, the Seals would open fire on them and kill as many as possible, then rush back to the shore and swim back to our boats and leave.

They told the two boat captains that they were to patrol up and down the river in front where the Seals were dropped off until they see three flares. One white, one red and one green. When they see those flares, the boats were to fire their 50 cal weapons at the shore between the White and Red Flares, as the Seals would be coming out between the Red and Green Flares.

They had a signal when swimming back so we would know the swimming sound were the Seals and not the VC. Peanut Butter is what we would say and they had to say Jam, or we were told to drop concussion grenades in the water, as the swimmers were probably VC.

The night of the operation came and there was no moon and quite dark. We loaded up the Seals and went down river to the rendezvous point and all the Seals dropped off, fully loaded with their special weapons, fully clothed, including boots on, and lead by their Lieutenant, which is always the case on these operations.

We did as instructed and began patrolling up and down the river using our radar as guidance. After about 45 minutes, we could hear and see several weapons firing, then a second barrage of firing, then silence. Soon, we saw only one flare on the shore, green. We couldn't fire for cover for fear of hitting the Seals.

After about twenty minutes we could here someone swimming towards our boat as we stopped the engines and floated. As the swimmer got near, the boat captain hollered out "Peanut Butter", but no answer, he hollered out again and then one more time, this time we heard a faint, "jam". We leaned over and grabbed the lone Seal and pulled him aboard. He said he don't know where everybody else is. We kept patrolling up and down and never heard any more swimming for the next hour.

After catching his breath, the loan Seal told us what happened. He said "we were there on the path waiting for the VC and saw about 5 or 6 of them coming up the trail, our Lieutenant signaled to wait until they were "front and center" then begin firing. They did just that, then, a minute later they encountered firing back at them from down the trail. Apparently, the VC traveled in two groups separated by 20 or 30 yards. So when the VC saw the firing of the Seals, they began shooting at the Seals. This guy said when the firing started he ducked down and started to crawl toward the bank of the river. After getting there he threw out the green flare and started to swim back to the boats, and that's all he knew. We didn't want to wait much longer, so we called in the Air Force C-130 to come and drop flares over the area. This took about twenty more minutes and we couldn't see anymore Seals either swimming or on the bank. We called off our patrol and went back to base.

The next day, the South Vietnamese Army and some Seals went to the area of attack and found 4 Seal heads sitting atop bamboo poles by the trail, but no bodies, not even the VC bodies. The village was empty also, and a lesson was learned about VC tactics.

One of the hardest thing for me was that I had to type the letters to the dead Seal families, without the details of the Top Secret operation, not even how they died and were was their bodies to be buried back home. As a side note, only each head was placed in a sealed casket and a name placed on the side. No family members were allowed to open the casket and the burial took place at the choosing of the family.

CHAPTER NINE

Operation "Robin Hood"

We had a Lieutenant Commander that came up with this idea to go to a VC village and shoot a lighted arrow into the grass huts and burn down the whole village. This meant I had to go back to Saigon Supply and order a Bow and Arrows. Talk about a peed off sergeant when he heard this request.

He got them from Japan and we went on a PBR down to an abandoned village to try them out. We put rags on the end of the arrow next to the point, then poured gas on it and lit it. Then the Commander, (who had a photographer from Stars and Stripes come along to take his picture while he was in cocked position) fired the arrow about 10 feet away. The arrow hit its target but soon the flame went out. After several tries, he got another idea, go back to the Army base and get a Flame Thrower. We got the flame thrower and went back and lit the shack on fire and took pictures. The commander was awarded a Bronze Star for his inventive idea. Part of the Scandal in the Jungle I have to report.

CHAPTER TEN

Operation 'Silver Spoon'

The next (fake operation) was again by the same Lieutenant Commander, was called "Silver Spoon". We had 10 PBR's go down to a known VC Village along the river in what was called "J" territory. The action was to have all ten boats run along the shore, one behind the other, and fire all our weapons at the hooch's. My job on the operation was to shoot the M-79 grenade launcher. Being an old duck hunter, I knew that there would have to be a lead time if I was going to hit the targets. So, the operation took place and I was very accurate with the grenades and it was neat to see the grenade(which looked like a 3 inch long and 2 inch around bullet) curve around to my right and hit perfectly on target. We made several passes and shot thousands of rounds of 50, 60, M-16's and my 30 or 40 grenades.

Then, we left and met in the middle of the biggest part of the river. The commander was on my boat and we went around to each boat and asked if they had seen any VC or taken any hits from the village. The answers were always the same, NO VC and NO hits.

We went back to base and the Commander wrote out his report for me to type and give to the Captain. I was totally shocked, it seemed we killed several VC and took as many as 15 to 20 hits to some of the boats, even a hole in our American Flag on our boat.

I finished typing the two page report and took it to Captain for his review and signature.

I walked into the Captain and laid the report in front of him and said "this is total BS". He said "what did I mean". I said," I was there and heard every Boat Captain say nothing every happened in return, just our firing our weapons". He said, "I'll take of it". The next thing I know about a month later we were having a command muster out front of the building and Captain Doolittle read a medal report of our operation and gave the Commander-in Charge of the operation a Silver Star for his actions. (Scandal in the Jungle)

CHAPTER ELEVEN

Motar's To No Where

This same Commander came up with another Idea of shooting a Mortar round from the boats to hit the villages. Again, I was the guinea pig. I was commissioned to take this 80 MM round mortar and hold it in my hands which another sailor dropping the round down the tube. I held it on the deck of the boat as the boat was moving away from the vacated island and aim it while the round was dropped. We did this and to my surprise, my bare hands started to burn (dumb move). I got some rags onboard the boat and dipped them in water and began the firing all over again. This proved to be a failure as I couldn't hit the island with any accuracy because of the motion of the boat and the guessing game I had to do with the aiming of the devise.

CHAPTER TWELVE

Shoot Out At The 'Ok Corral'

Sometime around May, two PBR sailors who had sent for and got their own pistols from home, were messing around aboard the LSD and were practicing "quick draw" with their pistols and one of them (apparently loaded gun) went off and hit the other sailor in the chest killing him. The Captain had to write a letter to his family that he was killed in action, and was awarded the "Purple Heart". (cover up).

CHAPTER THIRTEEN

Deadly Conseqenses

S everal times a year we had Retired Admirals and Captains come down to our operation to observe and be indoctrinated about our operations. This one time 3 or 4 of them came down and wanted to observe a "Fire Fight" by a PBR. The Captain asked two boats to go down to "J" territory and try to engage the enemy in a fire fight, so he and the retirees could observe this from a helicopter. Two boats volunteered with the man in charge, an Ensign, who was just new in country and never been aboard a PBR. Off they went and when reaching the 50 foot wide cannel just of the main river, they tried to engage the enemy by firing down both banks of this cannel but no action. So, the Ensign ordered his boat to go down in the cannel against the urgent call from the other boat "do not go in there its very dangerous". Well, he went down about 50 yards in and a Russian rocket went off and hit the metal guard plate, at the front of the twin 50 cal machine gun, which was moving from side to side. The force of the rocket took off the Ensign's head, the front gunner's head and the rear gunner went down. The other crew member grabbed his 60 cal machine gun and started firing but he too was cut in half by the VC 30 cal machine gun. This all happened in less than a minute and the boat was then set adrift further down the cannel.

The second boat fired all its weapons toward the shore and went back and forth at the head of the cannel firing. Because the cannel was so narrow, there was no way for the second boat to go down in and try to tow the other boat out. Well, the "boys" in the helicopter got what they asked for and then some. They called in the Air Force C-130 Dragon Ship and peppered the shore line several times. It wasn't until the next day after an all night vigil and flares being dropped, that the South Vietnamese Army came on one of their boats and landed on the land and march through the area to make sure it was clear in order to go down in the cannel and tow the boat back out. Only then did they see the total damage to the crew.

Again, the Captain had to call the Operation So & So and write letters to the dead family members. The Ensign was awarded the Navy Cross for his dumb action and he and the crew got Purple Hearts. Very few enlisted ever got medals for actions except for a few written about in other books. I will write about one sailor who got the Medal of Honor next.

CHAPTER FOURTEEN

My Hero

This is a story about Seaman David G. Ouellet, on 6 March 1967, serving with River Section 532, in combat against the enemy in the Republic of Vietnam. His PBR # 124 was making a high speed run along the Mekong River bank, and he was throwing hand grenades at the hooch's along the bank. When after pulling the pin on his grenade and reaching back to thro it, it fell from his hand and dropped to his feet. Realizing he only had 3 seconds after pulling the pin and releasing the clip, he shouted "Grenade" then shoved the Tail Gunner down and the grenade went off, destroying both engines and showering Seaman Ouellet with the remaining shrapnel.

His crew called for a helicopter and had him medivact'd to Binh Thuy Air Force Base for emergency treatment. This was a Sunday and I was just returning from my religious services on that base when the Radioman at our base got the call that the young man was asking to meet with a religious leader at the airport. Because I was the religion he needed, I rushed back over to the base to meet the helicopter. When it came in he was in a wire basket outside the chopper and I helped the crew carry him into a medical tent there on the runway.

As I was helping him in, I asked him what happened and he explained the incident as I previously reported.

After receiving medical help, he was flown to Tokyo where all critically wounded were sent. I did not see any external injuries that worried me about his condition so I wasn't too concerned about his future. While I was talking to him, he gave me his watch and asked if I would send it to his parents back home and I told him I would. I mailed the watch with a small note saying it didn't look too bad for him.

A month passed and the newspaper Stars and Stripes came out with a big head line "Navy Sailor put in for the Medal of Honor". After reading the story, I saw his crew had put him in for the Medal of Honor but the circumstances were not the same as he had told me.

They mentioned that an Enemy Grenade had been thrown into the PBR and David ran to the back of the boat and jumped on it to save his crew.

A month later, the paper came out again with a small story on the back page with the words "Navy Sailor denies he is a hero and don't deserve the Medal of Honor". I was happy he had told the truth.

Much later on, some 30 years, I found out he had died as the result of his injuries and he had indeed been awarded the Medal of Honor.

Despite the wording of the Medal award, he was still my Hero because he did push his crew member out of the way and took the rest of the explosion on himself, even if he tied to get out of the way.

CHAPTER FIFTEEN

Up Up And Away

One of my friends was an Air Force Spotter Pilot who flew a L-19 single engine Piper Cub. His job was to fly at about 3000 feet and spot Viet Cong positions so Jets could be called in and drop Napalm or other ordinance on their positions.

Lieutenant Evans asked me one day if I wanted to fly up to Saigon, from the Binh Thuy Air base where he was stationed, to take care of some personal business he had to attend to. Of course I said yes, as he figured I knew how to fly one of these Piper Cubs because I had told him I was once in the Civil Air Patrol as a kid.

We made out a flight plan and took off early in the morning. We had to sit on 3 flak jackets in case the VC shot at us as we flew over VC territory. The flight went well as I had taken off and flew to Tan Sa Nut air base, then the busiest air port in the world at that time. After getting within a couple of miles, he took over the controls and dove down through the clouds to make the landing.

After he finished his business, we took off again for home. Again, after he took off and got a few miles away from the Air Port, he gave me the controls. I had never landed a plane before, only flew them while I was in the Civil Air Patrol, so I was sure he would take the controls and land as we approached our home base, but he didn't. He only motioned from me to take her in. I quickly tried to remember how he had landed and kept the wings level with the nose level with the horizon, then as we got close to the runway, which was just across the river, I put down the flaps a little and cut the speed to about 80 knots. He adjusted the flaps a little and we were headed down across the river and when we were just 50 or so feet off the runway, a cross wind blew me off course. I quickly pumped the rudder pedals back and forth until I got the plane back on course just seconds before landing. I could see the controller in the tower lunge forward with his binoculars as he new I was in trouble.

There were sand bag pockets all along the runway on either side, where stacks of bombs and rockets were kept, so I had better not hit one of them.

Wham!, the plane hit down on the two front wheels and I pulled back on the throttle and the back wheel came down and we made it. I taxied over to the hanger where he kept his plane and shut her down. His first comment was, "wow, that was a rough one with the wind blowing us off course" I said "Yea, since I have never landed a plane before, that was a white knuckler for sure" He gasped and said "What!, you said you flew planes before" "Yes, flew, but I never said I ever landed one".

CHAPTER SIXTEEN

R&R (Rest And Relaxation)

All service members in Vietnam were allowed R & R, two in the country and one anywhere of their choice. I personally had four of them, two in a place called Vung Tau, about 30 miles north of Saigon next to the coastal area.

There was a hotel and other recreational areas in the town to go to. The hotel was pretty nice and had good food.

My first visit there, I decided to go to the beach. I was surprised to see a life guard there on a tower, because the water was very shallow. It was about one foot deep and a reef that went out about two hundred yards to the ocean. The life guard was an Army guy who was asked to be stationed there for his whole tour of duty because he was a Hawaiian and could be in the sun for long stretches without getting sun burned.

He had sent for an old 10 foot surfboard from home which he kept by the tower to rescue people. The only problem with that was that nobody ever went into the water because of the coral reef just under the water and it was hard to walk on let alone swim in. But, I could see some small waves, way out there, so I got talking to him about Hawaii and told him I surfed there and asked if he would let me take his board out there and try to catch a wave or two. He laughed but said go ahead and the board don't have any wax on top either.

Undaunted, I grabbed it and laid it in the water and with my tennis shoes on began walking along side the board pushing it out. Finally, after about a hundred yards the water got a little deeper and I could lie on it and paddle, very shallow paddle.

I reached the small waves, turned and caught one and actually stood up and went 50 feet and plopped down on the board so I wouldn't hit the coral. I paddled out two or three times and then walked the board back in.

The life guard was surprised, because he had never thought it was deep enough to surf. He said he was going out himself and give it a try.

The R&R was for only three days, so I just looked around the town, watched movies in the Hotel. I went back there one more time before I left Vietnam.

The other 1 week R&R out of country trip I took to Hawaii where I met my wife there. Some guys went to Australia, California, or wherever they wanted, the service paid for the trips and paid for a spouse (one way) trip to meet you. So, I had to pay for he to return back to the States when we were done in Hawaii.

While there in Hawaii, she and I visited relatives of hers and just went surfing and sight seeing around Oahu.

After I got back to the "War", several weeks later, an Army pilot came to our office and asked if anyone wanted to go for a one day visit the Con Son Island, off the coast about 100 miles for a little R&R. I said yes, and found out it was actually a prison camp where the South Vietnamese kept Viet Cong prisoners.

We flew over there and landed on the only air strip there close to the beach of one side of the island. Several of us that went on the trip went down to the beach and started swimming and started a fire to cook the hot dogs we brought with us. There was a real nice bay with a wrecked wooden ship sunk out in the middle of it.

One of the guys I was with talked me into to exploring the island. We went bare foot across the island pass the air strip to the other side of the island then started to circumvent the island back to our area. It was pretty hot on our feet so we had to jump from stumps of weeds all the way over to the beach where we could walk along in the water.

After about an hour of walking, we came upon this encampment which turned out to be the prison area for the VC. We kept our distance and walked on by so we wouldn't arouse any attention. As we went by, we saw a Vietnamese man fishing near the rocky beach. We engaged in very limited conversation with him and found out he was a VC who was allowed to go fishing and bring the fish back for the prisoners to eat.

We finally got back to the rest of the guys and related our experiences. All of a sudden, we looked down the beach and saw a female Vietnamese prancing in the water towards us wearing a bikini. A mirage? No! she was real and from a distance real good looking. Just as we thought we could go meet her and take a picture or twoooooo, an American came out of the bushes and caught up to her and began playing in the water with her.

We finally got enough guts and went over where they were and asked him what he was doing there and who he was. It turned out he was in the Coast Guard and stationed on that island with 4 other ship mates to watch the coast line for VC vessels. That's when we saw their small living quarters in the bushes and the tower and radio antenna. He said he met this girl in Saigon on R&R and she was half French and Vietnamese. He brought her to the island to live with him. He said he was going to marry her and take her back to the states when his tour was over.

CHAPTER SEVENTEEN

Maid Of Honor

Out of the blue, when the local male Vietnamese guards would bring the maids to the base to do their daily work, one of them walks in to my office dressed like a girl right out of the 50's, wide dress with several petty coats underneath. I asked her where she came from and where did she get that outfit? She said she just arrived from San Francisco and wanted job on the base. Her English was really good and she said she had been taken to the States several years ago by an American as his wife but, she wanted to come home to Vietnam and be with her family.

Somehow she managed to come back and here she was looking for a job. Of course I was able to help her with a job and she started doing the normal chores of washing clothes and cleaning the barracks. One day I found her sleeping on my bunk with another maid as it was Siesta time and there they were just as comfortable as can be on my bunk.

As an aside, most Vietnamese have their teeth overlaid with Gold, and as I found out, the more of their teeth that's covered in Gold the bigger their funeral would be when they die, an odd custom.

CHAPTER EIGHTEEN

Sunday Excursion

One Sunday, the Captain decided to play like a Navy Seal and took two boats and several men down the river to what we call "J" territory, which is a letter given for Viet Cong territory. He was dressed in an Aussie hat and carried an Aussie sub-machine gun. He also had someone following them with a movie camera to film their exploits.

They got to the area where they saw a Buda Temple in the jungle and pulled their boats onto the shore. The Captain jumps off and starts to walk towards the temple in a crouching position like he was looking to see some Viet Cong that he could shoot at. One of the men carrying the movie camera was walking behind him when all of a sudden the Captain tripped a wire booby trap and a grenade went off wounding him in his hip as he fell to the ground. The other men started firing their weapons towards the Temple and all around the area to scare off any potential enemy.

The wound in the Captain's hip wasn't very deep and big, but it was bleeding so one of the men put a hankie on the wound and they all went back to the boats and left the area. All this was caught on move film and the Captain awarded himself a purple heart medal.

He flew in world war II and the Korean War and was shot down twice and rescued but never received any wound that would qualify for a Purple Heart, which is a cut at least 1 inch long. So now, he had the wound and could give himself the medal.

The one big mistake the Captain made is he invited all the officers attached to 116 to come down to our base for their monthly meeting for combat instructions and reports which they would give to him each month. This time the two-star Admiral from Saigon came down to the meeting, which was not normal, as he was in-charge of all the PBR forces in country. The Captain had asked me to show the movie showing him getting his wound at this meeting, which I did.

I think the reason the Admiral came down was to see how the Captain was able to receive the Purple Heart, as a report was sent to the Admiral whenever someone was awarded any medals.

During the movie, the officers laughed and yelled when they saw what had happened to the Captain. After the meeting, they all laughed and slapped the Captain on the back and left. The Admiral didn't say anything as he just left and flew back to Saigon.

Two weeks later, a letter came from the Admiral to Captain Doolittle, which I opened up, as that was part of my job to screen all mail coming to the Captain, and WOW, the Admiral admonished the Captain for this action of parking the boats on shore and for him even being on the boats; and for his action with the machine-gun and getting wounded by tripping the booby trap. He was told he had disobeyed his orders and would be subject to disciplinary action.

After I had left Vietnam I found out that he would not be recommended for advancement to Admiral, which he was hoping for and that he was not allowed to come back to the United States for ten years. He was ordered to Japan to finish out the career before he could retire, and he would lose one rank to Commander. Especially during War Time, you can not disobey orders or else.

CHAPTER NINETEEN

Disobey Orders

Another time that an Officer disobeyed orders was when one day we had an American Army General down from Saigon to visit the Captain and when he was finished, the Captain's Chief Of Staff ordered this Lieutenant JG to call Saigon and get a helicopter ride for the General back to Saigon.

Well, to use a phone in Vietnam was like pulling teeth, the calls had to be routed through several phone banks and passed on, going through both American and Vietnamese systems.

Well, after about an hour of trying to get through to Saigon, the Lieutenant came over to me and told me to get on my phone and help him get through. I told the Lieutenant that my phone was for the use of the Captain and no one else. He told me it was an Order and I better obey his order or else. I did what I was ordered to do and began the process of calling. It took me over an hour to finally get through and ordered the chopper for the General.

About two hours later, a Vietnamese General walked through the door of our building and wanted to speak to Captain Doolittle. I told the Captain who was here to speak to him and he came out and asked the General in to his office and closed the door.

After thirty minutes or so, they came out shook hands and the General left. Then, the Captain asked me to come into his office. He asked me if I was on his phone for the last few hours, I said yes and explained why. He said Ok and as I left his office he yelled for his Chief of Staff to come in.

After he left the Captain's office he went back to his desk and started typing on his typewriter. After a few minutes he hollered out "Lieutenant so and so, front and center". The Lieutenant looked up from his cubicle and wasn't sure who had yelled at him. The Chief of Staff stood up and yelled at him again and the Lieutenant hurried over to his desk and stood there.

The Chief of Staff spoke loudly, "Stand at attention". The whole office was then looking over there to see what was happening. I of course had an idea what was going on, so I just sat there and listened. After the Lieutenant stood at attention for twenty or so minutes, the Chief of Staff looked up at him and told him "put in your papers, you are out of the Navy for disobeying my orders"

The Lieutenant JG had wanted to make the Navy a career so this was quite a blow. And, we all found out what it means to Obey your Orders, consequently, that's just what I did, but he didn't, as HE was supposed to get the helicopter, not me.

CHAPTER TWENTY

As Fate Would Have It

When anyone in the office wanted to go to Can Tho for a visit, they would check out a Jeep and go. One day an Officer checked out a jeep and went into town to some local pub. There he drank quite a bit and towards evening he got back in his jeep and headed back to the base in Binh Thuy.

As he drove through the town he ran over a Vietnamese woman killing her and kept on driving back to the base. The next day, a couple of Vietnamese Military Police came to our base and started looking at the front of a couple of jeeps setting there in front of our building.

They soon discovered blood and hair on the front bumper on one of the jeeps and came to talk to the Captain and explain what they were doing there; and wanted to know who had driven the jeep the day before.

After checking the log, it was discovered that this particular Lieutenant JG had taken it. The Captain called the JG to his office and found out it was him but he didn't remember ever running over anybody. The Captain put him on base arrest and told him to say in his quarters until we could have a Court Martial and resolve this issue.

I was told to prepare for the court and get everything ready for the next week. Meanwhile, the Lieutenant JG snuck out of his quarters and the front gate and made it a mile down to the Air Force base and went into the Officer's club they had on base. He got real drunk and started arguing with another guy and they went outside to the patio area. Soon the Lieutenant, who was about 6"6" tall and weighed about 250, was knocked down and hit his head on the cement patio. He was knocked out and in a coma when the medics arrived. He remained in a coma up in Saigon where he was taken and didn't look he would survive the injury.

So, the Captain called off the Court Martial and told the Vietnamese authorities what had happened and they were satisfied.

CHAPTER TWENTY ONE

Airforce Base Fire

One night while I was standing watch on the base, all of sudden mortar rounds started hitting the Air Force Base about a mile from us. I climbed up one of the comer towers to see what was happening. The barrage kept on for thirty or so minutes and it looked from a distance that several building were on fire.

I climbed back down and went to my watch station and just then the phone rang, I picked it up and someone on the other end said" Help, we need help" then that was it. I tried to get him back on the phone but there was no answer. I decided we might be able to help as all Navy personnel are trained in fighting fires while in boot camp. So, I ran around the base to each room and started knocking and hollering for men to come out and follow me. This was about 1:00 am in the morning and I only got about fifteen guys to come out. I commandeered a flat bed truck, told all the men to jump on and I drove over to the air base.

When we got there, the gate guard was missing and the phone was handing down. I drove through to the flight line where several helicopters were on fire. I saw a small fire truck near by with several holes in the tank and leaking water. I told several men to come with me and we grabbed the hose on the ground still connected to the fire truck.

We ran over to the first helicopter and started to pour water on the flaming mess. Soon I discovered we weren't doing any good as there were

Magnesium flares on board that can't be put out with water. So, I told several men to go over to the truck and follow me around behind the first hanger that was on fire.

When we got there, I noticed a fire hydrant on the road about 50 feet away, so I took the hose and a wrench I had taken from the truck, and ran over and hooked up the hose to the fire hydrant. Then, I told someone to turn on the hydrant after I got on the front of the hose. We had several guys on the hose as I knew the power would be pretty strong and would whip us around if we didn't all hang on to it.

I had more experience than any of the others, as I had fought range and mountain fires back in my home town when the fires would spark up by lightening during the summer.

I held the nozzle and the water was turned on and I aimed the water through a side window of the hanger to try to put out the fire. Little did any of us know, that there was a World War II plane in the hanger full loaded with ammunition that the Vietnamese would use to fly around the area and shoot at Viet Cong positions.

As we were trying to put out the flames, all of a sudden the ammunition starting exploding and I hollered for everyone to "hit the deck" and lie on the hose and cover your heads with your free hand. We didn't have helmets on and were dressed in our tee shirts and dungarees.

As we laid there, me holding the nozzle up to guide the water in through the window, the rest lying on the hose behind me, apparently we got enough water on the right spot, because the ammunition stopped exploding and we could then stand up and continue.

One airman who had come out of a bunker, who volunteered to help us, turned out to be an Officer without his uniform, only pants and tee shirt, so I didn't know who he was. After the fire was extinguished, he came up to me and asked who I was? I said, "I was a Yeoman (office worker)". He was in shock, he thought I was some commander, the way I was shouting orders and working the men the way I was. I told him I was the leading petty officer and we all had training in fighting fires, as does all Navy personnel.

He was very complimentary and told me to take the Sailors over to the mess hall and he would feed us steak and eggs for breakfast, as it was now 6:00 am.

We took him up on his offer, but when we walked into the chow hall, the chef in-charge got all upset that we would come into his mess hall dressed like that and all dirty. Immediately, the Officer rebuked the cook and told him we had just saved the base and for him to get busy and fry up some steak and eggs and anything else he had and to feed us all.

CHAPTER TWENTY TWO

On Patrol

I went on several patrols aboard the PBRs. This one instance we were down the Basac river and we noticed a sampan trying to avoid our patrol. We waved our hands at him then shot the M-16 across his bow to no avail. So, we took off after him to get lose enough to fire the twin fifties and not hit anyone else.

As we got closer, he headed for the shore and ducked into a small canal and disappeared. As we got close to the entrance of the small canal, we could just barley see the tip of his small sampan sticking out.

We couldn't go in after him so we decided to flag down a sampan coming down the river towards us. We got him close and through our interpreter, told him to paddle his sampan over there and bring out the other one we were chasing. The man said no, he was afraid, because he had his wife and kid with him. We let him go and waited for another one to come along with just one guy aboard.

One came along, we told him the same thing and he said no too. We told him if he didn't go in we would shoot him, he went in. Once he got in there he jumped out of his sampan and ducked down and ran somewhere. We didn't want to just shoot in there for fear of hitting someone on the other side of the canal.

We got another sampan coming down the river and this time he went in and tied on to the other sampan and brought it out. All that was in it was a pair of slippers and a small bag of rice, no weapons. The motor on the back of it had a hole in it which was probably one of our bullets from the M-16. We couldn't figure why he fled, unless he didn't have an ID, which meant he was either a VC or a Tax Collector.

Another patrol I was on, we came across several Vietnamese waving their arms at us from the bank. We went closer to see what was up and we saw this child hanging upside down from a tree. Apparently the VC had injured the child and hung him upside down by his legs. We had to get him down and medivac him to Can Tho for medical treatment. It turns out his was a common ploy to get us off the river so they could then run guns across the other side down river somewhere.

This is the reason we ordered several Boston Whalers to use them for these medivacs. Instead of taking off our patrol, we would call back to the base and they would send a Boston Whaler to do the pick up.

Most of the patrols were pretty routine, with checking IDs, looking for weapons and sweeping the tax collectors off the rivers. Night patrols were just watching the radar and patrolling all night, with some of the crew catching a few ZZZs.

This is the final chapter of my one year Vietnam experiences. As the book title indicates, this experience of watching these Naval Officers fake and then lie about their operations in order to get promotions and medals was very disappointing to me as an enlisted man who is supposed to look up to my superiors and even look forward to maybe someday becoming a warrant officer myself.

This is one of the reasons after nine and a half years I decided to get out of the Navy. No wonder one high profile Presidential candidate was able to throw away his medals in a protest of the war, as his own crew members noted, he lied about his activities so the medals really didn't mean that much to him.

Coming home we had a very nice ride on a Pan Am 747 instead of the C-141. But unlike today's returning service men and woman, there was no adoring crowds, no parades to welcome us home, only our own families.

Thanks a lot America, it was a pleasure to serve my country AND THE CAUSE OF FREEDOM.

To my surprise, I received two special medals of which I did not know I was put in for.

The first as indicated:

The Secretary of the Navy takes pleasure in presenting the Navy Achievement Medal to

Richard E. March
Yeoman Second Class

For services as set forth in the following:

"For outstanding achievement in the superior performance of his duties while serving with Commander River Patrol Force Staff from 5 Jan to 20 December 1967. Petty Officer Marsh distinguished himself by consistently carrying out his assigned duties with outstanding skill and resourcefulness, contributing significantly to a progressive increase in large volume of operation and administrative effectiveness. In addition to efficiently processing a large volume of operation and administrative task force correspondence, he voluntarily gave of his time to participate in the civic action program by teaching English classes for adult Vietnamese and in acting as a crew member on combat river patrol operations in the Mekong Delta region of the Republic of Vietnam. Petty Officer Marsh's leadership, professional ability and dedication to duty were in keeping the highest traditions of the United States Naval Service."

Petty Officer Marsh is authorized to wear the Combat "V"

For the Secretary of the Navy

JOHN J. LOWLAND
Admiral, U. S. Navy
Commander-in-Chief U.S. Pacific Fleet

Petty Officer Marsh is authorized to wear the Combat "V"

And the Second:

The Secretary of the Navy takes pleasure in presenting the Navy Commendation Medal to:

Yeoman Second Class
Richard E. Marsh
United States Navy

For services as set forth in the following:

"For meritorious achievement while serving with friendly foreign forces engages in the armed conflict against the Communist Insurgent (Viet Cong) in the Republic of Vietnam on 7 May 1967. Late that evening, Binh Thuy Air Base was struck by a barrage of over seventy rounds of seventy-five millimeter recoilless rifle by the Viet Cong. As a result, there were burning aircraft and hangers, leaking napalm bombs and flowing fuel from damaged aircraft. The entire flight line and base was in danger of destruction. Petty Officer Marsh voluntarily accompanied U.S. Naval personnel called for assistance. At the scene, he hastily organized his own fire team and led his group in hosing down a burning helicopter. Their clothes were set on fire frequently by ignition of fuel leaking from the helicopter, requiring a hosing down of each other. He ran to the front of a burning hanger, frantically searching for undamaged fire hoses and workable hydrants. Finding these, Petty Officer Marsh led four men to hooking up and directing water on the sides of the blazing hanger and adjacent buildings, despite the intense heat and small intermittent secondary explosions. Suddenly, a large quantity of twenty millimeter ammunition began to explode less than ten feet directly in front of them. For at least thirty seconds, he and his men maintained their prone positions with shrapnel fragments slicing through the air inches above their heads. After the explosions ceased, Petty Officer Marsh skillfully continued to lead his men in fighting the fire and effectively preventing the spread of combustion to adjacent buildings. After three hours of steady fire fighting, Petty Officer Marsh voluntarily remained behind with eight others to overhaul all the "hot spots". Petty Officer Marsh's extraordinary initiative, outstanding leadership, courage and sense of responsibility are in keeping with the highest traditions of the United States Naval Service."

Petty Officer Marsh is authorized to wear the Combat "V"

For the Secretary of the Navy

John J. Lowland, Admiral
United States Navy
Commander in Chief U. S. Pacific Fleet

You can bet your bottom dollar, I will never thro these medals away, even If I did not believe we should have been in that war.

ALOHA